SO-BED-964

Young Archaeologists

by Michael Cole
illustrated by Alan Flinn

Harcourt

SCHOOL PUBLISHERS

Requests for permission to make copies of any part of the work should be addressed to School Permissions and Copyrights, Harcourt, Inc., 6277 Sea Harbor Drive, Orlando, Florida 32887-6777. Fax: 407-345-2418.

HARCOURT and the Harcourt Logo are trademarks of Harcourt, Inc., registered in the United States of America and/or other jurisdictions.

Printed in China

ISBN 10: 0-15-351530-9
ISBN 13: 978-0-15-351530-9

Ordering Options
ISBN 10: 0-15-351214-8 (Grade 4 Advanced Collection)
ISBN 13: 978-0-15-351214-8 (Grade 4 Advanced Collection)
ISBN 10: 0-15-358120-4 (package of 5)
ISBN 13: 978-0-15-358120-5 (package of 5)

5 6 7 8 9 10 985 12 11 10 09

Characters

Narrator	**Leo**	**Professor Sonia**	**Lauren**
Rosa	**Victor**	**Alyssa**	**Max**

Setting: Camp Maya, an archaeology camp

Narrator: It's the first morning at Camp Maya. A group of fourth graders are sitting in a circle on the grass listening to Professor Sonia.

Professor Sonia: Good morning and welcome to Camp Maya! Over the next few days, you're going to learn what it's like to be an archaeologist.

Max: Are we really going to find things that are thousands and thousands of years old?

Professor Sonia: Absolutely! Under my guidance, my university students put together a site for you with objects from a Mayan town we excavated, or dug up, last winter. Does anyone know who the Mayans were?

Rosa: I know they lived a long time ago.

Professor Sonia: That's right. The Mayans lived in Central America. Their civilization flourished for centuries before their empire finally declined in the 1500s. They left behind a rich history, though. We've learned a lot about the past by finding their artifacts.

The Mayan Empire

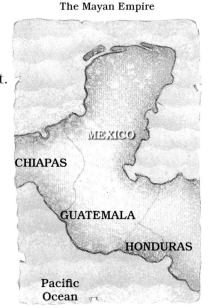

MEXICO

CHIAPAS

GUATEMALA

HONDURAS

Pacific Ocean

Alyssa: What's an artifact?

Professor Sonia: An artifact is an object from the past. Artifacts are usually in good condition because they have been protected by the mud. Artifacts were made by humans. Relics, on the other hand, are parts of once living things. For example, bones or teeth are relics. Now let's get to work.

Narrator: It's later that morning. Max holds on to the end of a tape measure. Rosa, holding the other end, paces along the edge of the dirt pit. Finally, she stops.

Rosa: That's exactly 18 feet (5.49 m) for this side.

Narrator: Max writes the information in a notebook as Lauren and Victor run over to them.

Lauren: Do you have all the measurements yet? We need them for the map of the site.

Max: We're almost done—I hope. This is an awful lot of work for a place that we're just going to dig up.

Professor Sonia: That's why we're doing it, Max. When archaeologists excavate an area, they essentially destroy it. Before they do that, they try to create a careful record of the place in its original, pristine state.

Narrator: The kids now work with Professor Sonia's university students to tie lengths of string to poles that are placed around the edge of the site.

Alyssa: This resembles a checkerboard.

Professor Sonia: It helps to divide the site into squares on a grid. That way we can easily keep track of where we find things. It also gives each of you a square to excavate.

Leo: These squares are really small. I can probably do about eight in one day.

Professor Sonia: I'm glad to know you're not timid about taking on a lot of work, Leo. However, I doubt you'll get through even one on your first day. Each square is going to require you to plunge deep into the depths of the Earth.

Narrator: It's the next morning. The kids work in small squares under the grid, digging in the dirt with trowels.

Lauren: I found something!

Narrator: Everyone rushes over to see.

Professor Sonia: Congratulations, Lauren, you're the first one to find something!

Lauren: It's a tile with a painting on it.

Professor Sonia: You're right, but it's only a small piece. What do you think that means?

Max: Obviously there must be more pieces.

Professor Sonia: That's what we hope. The first thing we do after we find something is create a record of how and where it was found. We measure how deep into the Earth it was buried and then draw a picture of it in its original position.

Victor: Archaeologists are constantly keeping records, aren't they?

Professor Sonia: The records are important because they help us reconstruct history.

Rosa: Professor Sonia, look at the soil here. It's a different color than the layer below it.

Narrator: The students gather around to look.

Professor Sonia: You'll find that as you dig, the soil may change color or texture. That's because, over thousands of years, new layers of soil have been piled on top of each other.

Leo: That means that the top is new, and the bottom layer is very, very old, right?

Professor Sonia: Exactly! The soil helps us tell the age of the objects we find. You undoubtedly know by now what that means you should do.

Max: Measure and keep a record of when the soil changes?

Professor Sonia: Right! Spoken like a seasoned archaeologist!

Narrator: The students are at work again the next morning. Alyssa and Victor hold pans full of dirt. The bottoms of the pans are made out of screens.

Professor Sonia: Now just shake the pan gently. Please don't hoist the dirt into the air. Once all the dirt has been shaken out, we'll see what's left.

Narrator: Alyssa and Victor shake the pans. Dirt falls out into another pan below them.

Victor: I didn't get anything. There are just some tiny pieces of glass left in here.

Professor Sonia: Victor, that's a tremendous discovery! It took a long time for humans to begin to make even simple tools. Glass-making shows that these were fairly sophisticated people. You probably won't find any more glass in the layers below where you found this glass because earlier people had not figured out how to make glass yet.

Narrator: Professor Sonia watches as Lauren and Max carefully try to fit pieces of tile together.

Lauren: I have to say, archaeology involves a lot more drudgery than I imagined. This is hard work.

Professor Sonia: It's not always fun. However, there are also moments you cherish when you find something wondrous. All the hard work becomes worthwhile, and you feel like it's a privilege to be an archaeologist.

Lauren: I felt that when I found the first piece of tile.

Professor Sonia: I'm glad to hear it. You know, other archaeologists have been studying Mayan art for a long time. They've figured out what some of the pictures and symbols mean. I have books that you can look at with their ideas. Maybe you can find out what the painting on the tiles mean.

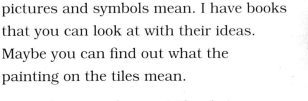

Max: That sounds great! Thanks!

Narrator: The next day, the students work in the lab in the archaeology department of the university.

Professor Sonia: Now that you've found all these objects, we need to take care of them. Everything has to be cleaned off, but we can't use water.

Leo: Why not?

Professor Sonia: Water might remove paint or even destroy some things. Remember, these are very fragile objects.

Rosa: What happens after they're clean?

Professor Sonia: We'll use chemicals to preserve them. Even air can attack these objects, like a predator eating away at them. I'll show you the steps we can take to save them.

Alyssa: I can guess what else we'll have to do—write up a record for each object.

Professor Sonia: Correct!

Narrator: Later that day, the group sits around a table together, looking at several objects.

Professor Sonia: The whole point of archaeology is to put together a picture of the past. To do that, you look at the objects you found and try to draw some conclusions. All of these objects were found together. What are they? What do they tell us?

Victor: That looks like a fish's jaw—a pretty big fish.

Professor Sonia: So what does that tell us?

Max: This place was once underwater?

Rosa: The fish was found with those pieces of pottery. There must have been people there at the time. I think we dug these up from someone's house. They were probably eating the fish.

Max: They couldn't keep fish in the refrigerator, though. They must have lived near the water.

Professor Sonia: Those are great ideas. What else?

Leo: There's something peculiar about that piece of wood. Doesn't it look burnt, as if it had been smoldering in a fire?

Alyssa: I know! They must have been cooking the fish! Didn't you tell us, Professor Sonia, that long ago people ate raw meat? These people must have lived after people figured out how to cook.

Professor Sonia: Correct! It looks like we found the garbage from someone's lovely, delectable fish dinner!

Kids: Yuck!

Professor Sonia: Archaeologists learn a lot from garbage! Look what we learned just now—how people ate, what they ate, and where they lived.

Narrator: The kids stand at tables, arranging the objects they found. Professor Sonia looks at their work.

Lauren: Look at my tiles, Professor Sonia. It looks like they tell a story about how the sun rises and sets each day. I couldn't find all of the symbols. I'd like to find them someday, though. I want to understand what the people were thinking and what they believed.

Professor Sonia: If you work hard and remain intrepid, I think you have a fine future as an archaeologist ahead of you—I think each of you do!

Rosa: Thanks, Professor Sonia! I'm going to write down what you said—just to keep a record of it!

Narrator: Everyone laughs.

Think Critically

1. Why are artifacts often in good condition when they are dug up?

2. What did the students conclude from the burned piece of wood?

3. Where did the Mayans live?

4. What is the main idea of this Readers' Theater?

5. Would you like to be an archaeologist? Why or why not?

🍁 Science

Discover Archaeology Look up more information about how archaeologists do their work. Write three paragraphs that describe their work. Make each paragraph about a different topic.

School-Home Connection Talk about some things you throw in the trash at your house. Discuss what an archaeologist might think they tell about your family.